Tintag

The place we now recognise as Tintagel, was more properly the strung out village of Trevena in the parish of Tintagel, nicknamed Tintagel Town. When the telegraph arrived here, the postal authorities adopted the name of the parish, and the name stuck. Originally known as *Boscyny*, or *Botcini*, after the ancient manor, it took its name from the exposed, craggy headland of *Dun Dagel*, signifying an impregnable fortress. This became corrupted into Tintagel. The little village which assumed the name of the parish had long been a place of some importance, and being closest to the parish church and to the castle, attracted early tourists.

A profusion of place names with the prefix *tre*, recall post-Roman times, when people gravitated from the old fortified villages to follow a freer life in isolated farmsteads across the windswept countryside. The word *tre*, indicating a farm, might be followed by a personal name, or be descriptive of its situation. Thus Treknow was a valley farm, Trenale a place on the moor, and Trebarwith a middle place. By the mid nineteenth century Trevena had become a self sufficient small village and focus of the parish, while Trenale, Trewarmett and Trebarwith were described as hamlets. The formerly important Bossiney was rated as a village, but by the end of that century all these settlements were regarded as villages.

The prefix *tre*

This Cornwall is very primeval: great, black, jutting cliffs and rocks, like the original darkness and a pale sea breaking in, like dawn. It is like the beginning of the world, wonderful: and so free and strong.
D.H. LAWRENCE 1916

A mid-nineteenth-century sketch of Trevena, when it was becoming the haunt of writers and artists.

The Nature of the Landscape

Silt and
sediment

The dramatic, rocky, windswept landscape that we see today began to form over 370 million years ago, as great quantities of silt washed down from high ground, and created soft sediments on the bed of a topical sea inhabited by small creatures. Over a vast

Tectonic plates

period of time, movements of the Earth's tectonic 'plates' carried these formations northwards to their present position, and they were to undergo a complete metamorphosis as the result of being overlaid by layers of heavy rocks, with later earth movements and volcanic action. For the tremendous heat and pressure caused the softer sediments to harden into topsy-turvy contortions, when the twisting, folding, tilting and buckling thrust some deeper layers of

Faults

rock to the surface, leaving some areas of weakness, known as 'faults'.

Glacial periods

The glacial periods during the past two or three million years, which caused some parts of the country to become buried beneath sheets of ice, brought extremely cold weather to this area, altering the nature of the vegetation, and putting further stress on the rocks. The melting of the ice caused the sea level to rise, scouring and deepening the inlets and river valleys, and eroding the frontier rocks of the coastline with relentless wave action. Some of those primeval marine creatures remain in the rocks as fossils, as if suspended in

Fossils

time, arousing our sense of wonder, and uniting us with life on Earth long before our own species existed.

Tintagel, in early days, was the gateway into the Celtic peninsula, the only military road passing it on its course along the north coast of Devon and Cornwall. Hence its ancient importance, and the battles which occurred in its immediate vicinity. The boundary of the Celt and Saxon may still be traced from the Tamar to Tintagel by the names of the villages – Michaelstowe, Jacobstowe, Davidstowe, Morwenstowe &c. . . '.

MURRAY'S HANDBOOK OF DEVON & CORNWALL 1865

Prehistory

The earliest people to venture this way were probably nomadic hunter gatherers, who left no enduring mark upon the landscape. Archaeological evidence suggests that the nearby high granite moors were quite heavily populated in prehistoric times, when the climate was more favourable for gleaning a livelihood, and that these communities gravitated to the moorland fringes and beyond as the weather conditions deteriorated. Although the area around Tintagel is dotted with tumuli and ancient earthworks, many traces of our early ancestors have been lost beneath the plough, as happened with the Iron Age encampment above Trenale.

Plan of Bossiney Castle, based on a mid-nineteenth-century interpretation.

A network of roads linked the commanding hill fortresses of north Cornwall, and ancient routes converged on the natural coastal stronghold of Tintagel Island. Condolden Barrow, to the south-east, and the old motte castle at Bossiney were focal points along the way. There was a diversion to Bossiney Cove, where attempts had been made to create a viable haven for shipping. The fortified headlands of Tintagel, Barras and Willapark formed part of a defensive chain along this steep, dramatic coastline.

The Romans left some intriguing evidence of their association with these parts, including two milestones. One was serving as a coffin rest and unofficial sharpener of reaping hooks at the lower entrance of Tintagel churchyard until 1889, when a perceptive observer caught sight of some lettering thrown into relief by the angle of the setting sun, and realised that it might be of some significance. It was found to bear an inscription to the Emperor Caesar Gaius Valerius Licinius, dating from around 250 AD. A second milestone was being used as a gatepost at Trethevy, 1 1/2 miles to the northeast, when it was discovered in 1919. It bore an inscription to the Emperors, Caesars and Lords Galius and Volusian, who reigned briefly between 251 and 253 AD.

The Romans

The discovery of these milestones and of coins and imported pottery dating from the third or fourth century, which appear to align with various records, suggest that the headland of Tintagel was a focal point of some importance in Roman times, recognised by the Imperial authorities, and serving perhaps as a local tax centre. Assuming this to be the case, the inhabitants of this windswept headland at that time would have enjoyed high quality, imported domestic goods, and some other satisfying spin-offs, unknown to the rest of the population.

The importance of Tintagel headland

When the Romans departed, sections of Britain fragmented into small kingdoms, and this area had its own petty king based originally in the 'old court' at Helstone, near Camelford, and later at the 'new court' at Lesnewth. During this more settled period people gravitated from their fortified villages to homesteads and tiny settlements scattered across the countryside, and we can see this pattern of isolated farmsteads on the Ordnance Survey maps of today. Tintagel is now thought to have been a royal stronghold and place of some importance in the early sixth century, where archaeological discoveries indicate cultural and trading links with Byzantium. There were movements of population from Ireland and Wales and between Cornwall and Brittany over the next few centuries, in an age of Celtic saints.

The Roman milestone found at Trethevy.

The Impact of Invasion upon the Landscape

The Saxons

The arrival of the Saxons destroyed these tribal kingdoms and created much strife in Cornwall, although they did not make as much impact on the traditional way of life around Tintagel as in some other places. Intriguingly, a tenth century cross bearing an inscription to the effect that it was set up by Aelnat for the good of his soul, was discovered at Trevillet Farm by one of Lord Wharncliffe's stewards in the late nineteenth century. Having served its time propping up a gate, it was removed and placed in a prominent situation outside the Wharncliffe Hotel, where it remains.

The Normans

After the Norman Conquest in 1066, many of the Cornish manors were seized by King William, who set his half brother Robert, Earl of Mortain, to oversee them, and embarked on the Domesday survey. In order to hang on to the territory they had taken over, the Normans constructed a number of formidable and intimidating castles, like those of Launceston and Trematon. The stronghold at Bossiney was of the simpler, circular bank and ditch type, which would have incorporated a surveillance tower, and housed a small garrison. There would have been a wooden ramp across the ditch, and a secure, guarded gateway. This was superseded by the mighty and commandingly positioned castle built on Tintagel Island in the thirteenth century.

The bold promontory on which the castle was built had been recognised as a natural stronghold from time immemorial, and successive generations incorporated the existing coastal features and rock formations in their construction work so deftly, that it is difficult to differentiate between art and nature amidst the romantic ruins that we see today. When the elevated headland was first fortified, the neck of land linking the 'island' to the mainland would have been more substantial, and the narrowing of the isthmus, brought about by the pounding action of the waves, prompted the builders of the medieval castle to extend the mainland section. Erosion will eventually create a true island.

Tintagel Island

The Roman legacy

The Roman presence had left a prestigious stamp on the exposed clifftop site, and when Cornwall became part of the west country kingdom of Dumnonia, the choice of Tintagel as a royal seat for kings visiting this part of their domain, may have been influenced by a desire to harness some of this reflected glory. Excavations have revealed larger quantities of pottery and other artefacts relating to post-Roman times, than have been discovered anywhere else in Britain, and the nature of these top quality imported goods would suggest that Tintagel was once the scene of lavish hospitality and grand ceremonial in the style of ancient Rome, in a spectacular Cornish setting. Trading vessels would have unloaded in the natural little haven at the foot of the cliffs between the Island and Barras Nose, with the site providing its own security.

At some point in the fifth or sixth century a decision was made to reinforce the Island stronghold by excavating an enormous ditch along a natural fault line, and constructing a strong defensive wall with the material. This gave rise to the name of *Din Tagell*, meaning a fortress with a narrow entrance. Geoffrey of Monmouth described this constricted access rather fancifully as being 'through a strait rock, which three men shall be able to defend against the whole power of the kingdom'. It is not surprising that this impressive site, surrounded by colourful legends, was harnessed by successive seekers-of-power.

Earl Richard's castle

The Arthurian connection

Perhaps it was a desire to be associated with the legendary heroic and idealistic splendour which had fallen on Tintagel's earlier castle walls, which influenced Earl Richard's decision to construct a new castle here in AD 1233. For the twelfth-cptury writer Geoffrey of Monmouth had linked the site with a Cornish duke, Gorlois, and the conception of a child by means of deception and magic, destined to become the great King Arthur. This famous fable had been much embellished by that time, and the ambitious Earl, who was the brother of King Henry III, may well have felt that it would enhance his image here and in Europe if some of the glory were to rub off on him.

One of the main features of Earl Richard's splendid castle, built on steep terrain, was the construction of courtyards on the mainland

and the Island. These were major engineering projects, for apart from clearing away existing structures, the terraces had to be built up, the land levelled and held in place by a retaining wall. It was something of a triumph of man over nature, guaranteed to impress and enhance one's status. The mainland courtyard was a reception area, where the visiting Earl and guests arriving on horseback would dismount, and be welcomed in ceremonial style by guardsmen and officials, with grooms and servants standing by. The courtyard would have incorporated a guardroom, storerooms and other buildings, while latrines set in the outer walls were designed to empty directly over the cliffs. The Great Hall in the Island courtyard was the hub of business life and formal entertaining, and there would have been adjoining domestic areas for the preparation of food. A very well ventilated underground tunnel a short distance away may have served as a cool food store. These heavy buildings put a tremendous strain on the made-up land, and the retaining walls had to be buttressed to rectify the situation. The Island had the advantages of a reliable water supply, good grazing land, scope for limited cultivation in devised protective areas, and a defended wharf, but there was always some degree of reliance on the mainland.

Although the building of the castle may have been the realisation of an idealistic dream, Earl Richard does not appear to have visited Tintagel very often, and subsequent earls took little interest in the place. The fabric started to deteriorate soon after his death in 1722, and things went rather quiet around this island haunt of jackdaw, gull and Cornish chough thereafter. The castle subsequently became the property of the Crown, and it was committed to the custodianship of a succession of county sheriffs. Much of the land was let out for grazing, and there were rights of Free Warren.

The Castle and its Legends

An impressive ruin

The castle had become an impressive ruin by the time the antiquarian John Leland visited the area in 1538. He observed that, 'This Castelle hath bene a marvelus strong and notable forteres, and almost *situ loci inexpugnabile*, especially for the Dungeon that is on a great and high terrible cragge environid with the Se . . .'. He went on to say that large sections of the weather-beaten, ruined castle had slumped into the sea as the result of erosion, and that the headland had almost become an island. Although there had previously been a drawbridge, the only access to the Island at that time was by means of a bridge fashioned from long elm logs. He also mentioned the pretty chapel of Saint Ulette, tombs, vaults, a well, and quadrant walled area like a garden plot. He concluded by saying, 'The Grownd of this Isle now nuryshyth Shepe and Conys' (rabbits).

The famous headland and castle remain in the ownership of the Duchy of Cornwall, and are managed by English Heritage.

Fables, myths and legends

A profusion of colourful fables, myths and legends, with their roots in oral history, seem to have filled a void left by scanty docu-

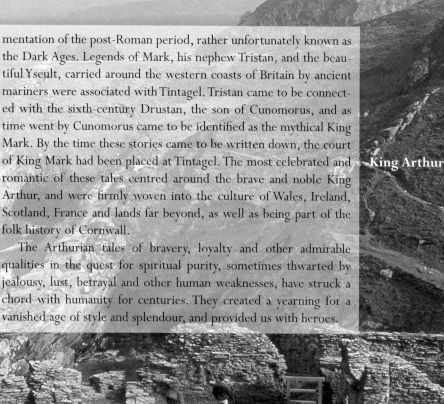

mentation of the post-Roman period, rather unfortunately known as the Dark Ages. Legends of Mark, his nephew Tristan, and the beautiful Yseult, carried around the western coasts of Britain by ancient mariners were associated with Tintagel. Tristan came to be connected with the sixth-century Drustan, the son of Cunomorus, and as time went by Cunomorus came to be identified as the mythical King Mark. By the time these stories came to be written down, the court of King Mark had been placed at Tintagel. The most celebrated and romantic of these tales centred around the brave and noble King Arthur, and were firmly woven into the culture of Wales, Ireland, Scotland, France and lands far beyond, as well as being part of the folk history of Cornwall.

King Arthur

The Arthurian tales of bravery, loyalty and other admirable qualities in the quest for spiritual purity, sometimes thwarted by jealousy, lust, betrayal and other human weaknesses, have struck a chord with humanity for centuries. They created a yearning for a vanished age of style and splendour, and provided us with heroes.

Distinguished Residents

Important families

Important families in the history of the parish include the Wades of Trethevy, who played an influential role in local life for about 300 years, the Woods of Trevillett, who were landowners, jurors and members of Parliament, and the Wharncliffes, who once owned most of the parish lands, but sold out in 1911. Parishioner John Bray found social advancement through marrying the maid of William Pitt's wife, for this connection gained him a lucrative contract to supply horses to the army in the wartime context. The fortune thus acquired allowed him to build a fine residence at Downrow, which he called Trebray.

Visitors

Street scene showing Trevena House, which was later to become King Arthur's Hall, and the adjoining Wharncliffe Hotel, c.1870s.

Trevena attracted many distinguished visitors in the nineteenth century, including John Douglas Cook, the editor of the *Morning Chronicle* and founder editor of the *Saturday Review*. He spent the summer of 1860 here, living initially in a little cottage by the church, then building the prestigious Trevena House, which later became incorporated in King Arthur's Hall. He was a noted gourmet, and enjoyed entertaining local clerics. He died in 1868, and was buried in the churchyard. Trevena House subsequently belonged to Sir Arthur and Lady Hayter, who entertained distinguished guests on their occasional brief visits to Tintagel. This house now forms part of King Arthur's Great Halls, a Grade II listed building. The millionaire Frederick Glasscock, who was inspired by the Arthurian ideals, erected the Hall of Chivalry and King Arthur's Hall in the 1920s, and the building was further extended and enhanced in the 1930s.

Stylish transport outside the Wharncliffe Hotel c. 1910, by which time another storey had been added, to cope with demand from increasing numbers of tourists.

An advertisement from Kelly's Directory, 1910.

The Wharncliffe Hotel,

TINTAGEL, CORNWALL.

Re-furnished, Re-decorated, and under entirely New Management.

THE old-established Hotel of the locality, replete with every convenience for the visitor.
Cosy and comfortable, and situated in one of the few remaining seaside resorts of the country that have not been wrecked by the vandalism of latter day innovation.

The Hotel is near the King Arthur's Castle of romance, on the picturesque coast that gave inspiration to Tennyson, Irving and Hawker, unparalleled for the rugged grandeur of its cliffs, and full of historical and legendary interest.

'Buses from the Hotel meet the principal trains at Camelford Road Station, and special trains are met on receipt of telegram addressed "DERRY, TINTAGEL," or post card. For visiting Roughtor and Brown Willy, and the many other places of interest mentioned in the Guide Books, carriages may be obtained at the Hotel.

From November 1st till Easter, Parties of Visitors for a week, numbering not less than two, will be entitled to a drive to any places of interest within 10 miles without charge.

ACCOMMODATION FOR MOTORISTS.   HEADQUARTERS OF THE AUTOMOBILE ASSOCIATION.
——— GOLF LINKS WITHIN A FEW MINUTES' WALK. ———
BATHING OF THE BEST & SAFEST IN THE IMMEDIATE LOCALITY.   CUISINE OF THE BEST.

Terms Moderate, and considerably reduced during the six months following the 1st October, when the locality is highly recommended to persons desiring mildness and salubrity of climate.

Proprietors : Wm. DERRY & SON, Ltd.,
Tariff List sent on application.   *Agency for the London & South Western Railway Co.*

The imposing entrance to King Arthur's Great Halls, where the public can savour the Arthurian experience.

King Arthur's Castle Hotel, designed by Silvanus Trevail, was erected in 1899, and is now a Grade II Listed Building. The original plan to build it on Barras Nose, led to that headland being purchased by local people and being handed over to the National Trust as their first coastal acquisition.

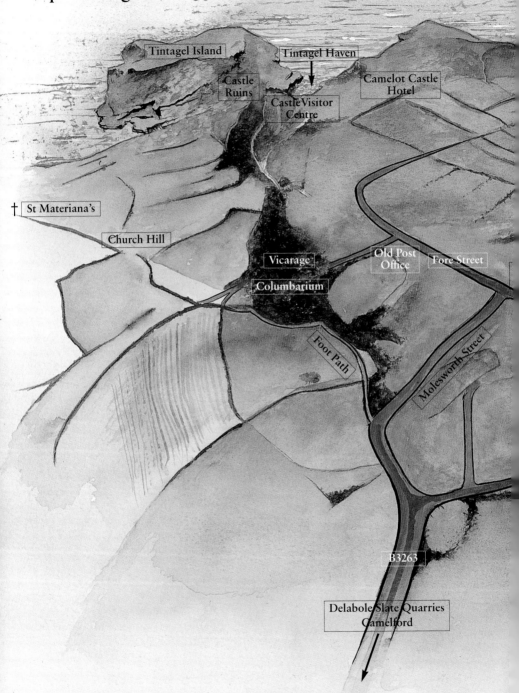

Map of Tintagel showing places named in the text

Tintagel Island

Tintagel Haven

Castle Ruins

Camelot Castle Hotel

Castle Visitor Centre

† St Materiana's

Church Hill

Vicarage

Old Post Office

Fore Street

Columbarium

Foot Path

Molesworth Street

B3263

Delabole Slate Quarries Camelford

Bossiney Cove

N

thur's
ls

TREVENA

Bossiney Road B3263

Tintagel Visitor Centre

Mining and Movement

Transportation of slate

In the nineteenth century small trading vessels came to Tintagel Haven to be loaded with slate, by means of an ingenious and picturesque system of overhead derricks and pulleys. But all too often the treacherous groundswell and thunderous waves in this confined area would smash a boat to pieces before it had a chance to get safely afloat on the rising tide.

Other mineral workings

There was intensive slate quarrying along this section of coast extending inland to the still operational Delabole Quarry (see page 18). It had long been known that a number of promising mineral lodes containing silver lead ore, copper and zinc traversed the area of Tintagel Head and the Island, and the western end of Trevena village became cavernous with manganese workings. There was a brief attempt to exploit lodes on the headland in 1853, and about 20 years later a determined effort was made to extract the valuable ores which lurked beneath the former domain of King Arthur himself. As the Duchy had stipulated that there should be no surface scarring in the vicinity of the castle, an adit (horizontal tunnel) was created in

Engraving by George Cooke – after the painting by J.M.W. Turner, 1818, published by Cooke, 1849.

Bringing vessels into Tintagel Haven, c. 1875. Loading with slate was a hazardous, labour intensive exercise, requiring local knowledge and a great deal of skill.

the cliffs near the entrance to Merlin's Cave, from which a shaft was sunk. This mining endeavour gave rise to a small complex on the northern side of the Trevena Stream, including an office, and carpenters' and blacksmiths' shops. However, this optimistic venture turned out to be rather short lived, and the entrance to King Arthur's mine was bricked up.

Vessels were 'hobbled' into the haven of Tintagel, using a system of towing in with rowing boats and carefully controlled warping with ropes and bollards.

Delabole slate being loaded at Port Gaverne, c. 1880.

Quarrying activity

The quarries present one of the most astonishing and animated scenes imaginable. The traveller suddenly beholds enormous pits, which, excavated by the un-interrupted labour of centuries, are encompassed by dark blue hills of rubbish, continually on the increase, and slowly encroaching upon the domain of the farmer. The scene is enlivened by a throng of men busily engaged in various noisy employments, while waggons and horses are everywhere in rapid motion, and steam engines are lifting with a harsh sound their ponderous arms, and raising loaded trucks from the depths of the pit, or masses of slate of several tons' weight, which are seen slowly ascending guide-chains to stages which overhang the quarries. . . .

MURRAY'S HANDBOOK OF DEVON & CORNWALL 1865

An aerial view of the far-famed Delabole Slate Quarry in June 2000, where modern technology produces much slate with a minimal workforce.

The world famous quarries at Delabole, just 4 miles to the south of Tintagel, are of great antiquity, and have long enjoyed the reputation of producing the finest slate in the kingdom. Although nobody knows exactly when the quarrying activities began, the documentation of the name *Delyou Bol* in 1284, indicating a pit, demonstrates that the exploitation of slate was being carried out before then. In his *Survey of Cornwall* published in 1602, Richard Carew described the roofing slates as being 'in substance thinne, in colour fair, in waight light, in lasting strong'.

This isolated stack at Lanterdan Quarry was left by the quarrymen because of its inferior quality slate. This quarry was being worked in the mid seventeenth century.

In the mid nineteenth century about 1,000 men were being employed at the three pits, which were later merged into one gigantic excavation, earning the reputation of the biggest man-made hole in Britain. At that time roofing slates, cisterns and other products were being exported to various parts of the United Kingdom, France, Belgium, the West Indies and America, from Port Gaverne and Boscastle. Traditionally, the slates were split into standard sizes known as *Ladies, Countesses, Duchesses, Queens, Rags* and *Imperials*, and their quality could be discerned by the sound when struck, the colour and the feel. Fine specimens of fossils, including the famous Delabole Butterfly, and sparkling rock crystals known as Cornish Diamonds have been found in these quarries. The work of centuries continues today, with the emphasis on producing decorative fireplaces and other high quality artefacts, and the public can enjoy a visit to 'the oldest and largest working slate quarry in England'.

Slate exports

The fossil Spirifer Verneuilii, *commonly known as the Delabole Butterfly, on account of the wide valves resembling wings.*

TECHNOLOGY FOR
THE FUTURE
*The Delabole Wind
Farm and Gaia Energy
Centre aim to show the
benefits of renewable
energy.*

Industrial archaeology

*Trebarwith Strand
c.1890, where vessels
were loaded with slate,
and sand was collected
for use on the land.*

The great demand for slate gave impetus to the establishment of a number of quarries between Delebole and Tintagel, including Penpethy, Bolehill, Bowithic, Jeffray's Pit, Trebarwith and the Prince of Wales Quarry, where visitors can follow the quarry and engine house trail, and enjoy the wildlife which has colonised the old workings. Inland quarries always had problems in disposing of overburden and waste material from the operations, but the rocks tended to be conveniently exposed on a string of nearby cliff edge workings, where any unwanted material could be dumped into the sea. Furthermore, coastal quarries had the advantage of shipping out stone direct, instead of having to convey very heavy loads over the rough North Cornish roads.

All along the coast between Tintagel and Trebarwith Strand there is evidence of former quarrying activity, now much cherished as industrial archaeology. There were tramways, tunnels, masts, cranes, cables, winches, pulleys, platforms, flights of ladders, steep stairways and an array of work-a-day buildings, all playing a vital role in the production and export of slate from the clifftops. The quarrymen who toiled in this awesome environment risked life and limb every day, and accidents happened all too frequently. One of many such accidents occurred during boring operations in April 1889, when a section of rock collapsed into the sea carrying three men to their deaths. The disaster cast a gloom over the whole parish, and great sympathy was felt for the bereaved. At Lamb's House Quarry the men had to make a descent down the cliff face to reach the quarry

entrance, and after yet another tragedy, the *West Briton* newspaper asked why the Mines Regulations Bill had not embraced the slate quarries, pointing out, 'If the visit of an inspector is necessary at a mine it is equally so at a slate quarry.'

The Haven at Tintagel

The character of this iron-bound coast is well seen at Tintagel. The sea front, mostly composed of slate, presents a series of inaccessible headlands and gloomy recesses, illustrating the influence of the 'Atlantic drift', which is especially directed into the Bristol Channel. The sea is here ever heaving in long undulations, and the water being deep to the land, the base of the cliffs is worn by the roll of the waves into a concave surface, which presents an effectual barrier to escape in shipwreck.

MURRAY'S HANDBOOK OF DEVON & CORNWALL 1865

The haven at Tintagel must have played a vital role in keeping the fortress viable. Cargoes were despatched on the defended wharf by the Iron Gate, or landed on the sandy beach. In 1583, when there were fears of a Spanish invasion, Sir Richard Grenville reported: 'From the sea there are two landing places; against one of them is a wall with a gate in it, called the Iron Gate; this wall is of lengthe one hundred and twenty foote, in thickness five foote, garrated, now somewhat ruinal; which was in old time sufficiente for the defence of that place. . . . By the workes without this wall (beinge the landing place), four or five of the greatest sortes of shippes may, with most windes, ride, and lay their sides to the workes and land anie companie of men; the water being ther at the lowest ebb five fathom deep, and the ground in this bay before the rockes faire and sandy for a moringe.'

Quarrymen working at Long Grass Quarry c.1934. The quarry closed in 1937.

'Donkey boys' loading sand for agricultural use at Trebarwith Strand in the early 1900s.

The Parish Church

Tintagel's windswept, salt-sprayed churchyard has been the final resting place for many a shipwreck victim along this awesome section of coast.

The church of St Materiana, in its dramatic maritime situation on the clifftop just south of the Island, is one of the most ancient and interesting in the county. The building that we see today occupies a site of great antiquity, where earlier churches had stood. Unfolding archaeological evidence has revealed that this was an early burial site, possibly dating from the sixth century, when the Island was a royal stronghold. An array of pottery and other fascinating artefacts have been discovered here, and this clifftop site undoubtedly harbours many more secrets.

This early Norman church bears traces of the Saxon style, and has been restored and enlarged at various times. Not surprisingly, the roof and fabric have taken a series of batterings from the Atlantic storms throughout the ages, and at one time netting was placed between the rafters to protect the worshippers from falling debris.

The church of St Materiana in its isolated clifftop position, where a section of the churchyard is set aside to provide a haven for wild flowers and insects.

About a century ago attempts to fly the flag of St George from a flagstaff on the turreted tower had to be abandoned, when the pole was struck by lightning. The following day one of the bells was dislodged from its bearings, but fortunately it was retrieved from the floor undamaged and replaced.

Flying the flag on the tower

The benefice was first documented in 1259, when it was appropriated by the Monastery of Fonterault in Normandy. The incumbents were taxed by the monastery, and lived on their portion of the local tithes, together with whatever profits they might make from their small glebe tenement. The buildings were adapted and extended at various times, and the complex came to include a range of outhouses, set in gardens and orchards shielded from wind and weather by protective belts of trees. Apples, hops and other crops were grown in the gardens, where there was also a columbarium (round,

The benefice linked with Normandy

Feeding the clergy

This circular, dry stone columbarium incorporated 247 nesting holes for domestic pigeons, thus providing a reliable supply of meat and eggs.

stone-built pigeon house), for the breeding of pigeons for the pot, to supplement their diet of salted fish and meat through the bleak winter months. They kept oxen, cattle, pigs and poultry, and had specifically designated areas for producing malt, beer and dairy foods.

The later vicarage house in the valley between the village of Trevena and the church, is surrounded by an ancient, lofty wall, and entered through a large gateway beneath a four centred arch. The handsome columbarium remains in the garden.

The church of St Materiana has served as a conspicuous landmark for seafarers for centuries. The five bells which sang out from its distinctive square tower was the envy of the folk of neighbouring Boscastle, who wanted some bells for the silent tower of their church at Forrabury. The story goes that the ship carrying these precious bells from London was wrecked on the rocks to the north of Tintagel, and that eerie subterranean bells can be set a-ringing during wild Atlantic storms.

The old tradition of seeking sanctuary in a church was embraced by John le Waleys in 1317. After confessing to a theft, and asking for a string of other offences to be taken into consideration, the coroner ordered that the two pence in his possession be confiscated, and allowed him to deport himself from the king's realm.

One of the most enduring personalities here was Charles Chillcott, who was Tintagel's answer to the Cornish Giant of Stratton. Giant Chillcott's vital statistics demonstrate that his girth exceeded his height, for he measured 6 feet 9 inches around the chest and stood 6 feet 4 inches in his stockinged feet. He weighed in at about 460 pounds. His massive thighs were a yard and 4 inches in circumference, and his stockings had the capacity to hold 6 gallons of wheat. This famous pipe-smoking gargantuan personality enjoyed his notoriety, and when curious folk called to see him was in the jovial habit of saying, 'Come under my arm, little fellow!' He died of an apoplectic fit in April 1815, at the age of 60.

St Nectan's Glen and the Rocky Valley

St Nectan's Glen and the Rocky Valley lie just beyond Bossiney, on the road to Boscastle, and walkers can take footpaths up the wooded valley to the waterfall known as St Nectan's Kieve, or northwards down a delightful, flowery valley, which makes its rugged way to the coast past two old watermills. The upper part of the Trevillett Valley is well wooded, with a narrow chasm, in which a waterfall cascades through a cleft in the high vertical rock face into a naturally occurring basin or kieve. This magnificent hanging valley, noted for its multifarious mosses, supports a wide range of vegetation and a colourful array of flowers, much favoured by the butterflies. The atmosphere become aromatic on a dreamy summer's day, as the rocks absorb the heat, and the plants release their subtle scents. Having created gullies, cateracts and whirlpools, the bold Trevillett stream encounters a final gorge before pitching dramatically into the sea.

A hanging valley

This functional and pleasing mill in the Rocky Valley was an inspiration to the artist Creswick.

The haunting beauty of St Nectan's Kieve attracted a host of nineteenth-century poets and dreamers. The place was associated with a wealth of myths and legends, about King Arthur and his Knights of the Round Table, monks, nuns and mariners, ghosts and pixies. According to tradition, a ruined building above the waterfall was the chapel of St Nectan, a hermit who found spiritual inspiration here for many years. The story goes that a tall tower with commanding coastal views which once stood behind the chapel, housed a silver bell, used perhaps

The mysterious maze rock carvings on a rockface adjacent to the lower mill in Rocky Valley bear a striking resemblance to the Minoan style of Ancient Greece, and are thought by some people to date from the Bronze Age.

Rugged Bossiney Cove, where sand used to improve the soil was hauled up on the backs of donkeys.

Facing page:
The waterfall at St Nectan's Glen is not only a Site of Special Scientific Interest. According to legend the Arthurian knights were baptised here before setting off on their quest for the Holy Grail.

to warn local seafarers of impending dangers. The pious man apparently was wont to disagree with passing strangers on religious matters, and shortly before his death he decided to dispose of the bell in the deep recesses of the waterfall, so that non-believers would never get their hands on it, and requested that he be laid to rest within splashing range of his beloved waterfall. Centuries later some foolish miners made attempts to recover the silver bell. However, they took to their heels and fled when an eerie voice warned them, 'The child is not yet born who shall recover this treasure.'

Tintagel's famous Old Post Office in 1902, which is now in the care of the National Trust. This was a basic fifteenth-century dwelling, with upper chambers and extensions created at later dates.

A street scene in 1910, demonstrating the slate roofs and chimneys which are so characteristic of these parts.

A Cornish hedge in the distinctive 'curzyway' style.